THE BLUE SKY PRESS • AN IMPRINT OF SCHOLASTIC INC. • NEW YORK

MY
LIGHT

by Molly Bang

When you see the city lights at night,
they look like stars have fallen down to earth.

Those lights ARE starlight—my light.

I am your sun, a golden star.

You see my radiance as light.

Each day I warm
your land and water.

Tiny drops of warm
water rise and
form clouds.

The clouds cool down.

My energy falls in rain.

The water flows
from streams to
rivers, carrying
my energy
down,
down,
down.

A dam!
You humans stop the flow.
My energy is trapped.

Whish!
Some water shoots down
tunnels to giant turbines.

Whoosh!
The water spins the
turbines round and round.
It spins my energy to
generators, which
make electricity.

Now my energy is in
the electricity. It flows
away in copper wires.

The wires hum!

Electricity flows,
pulsing, pulsing, pulsing
my energy out
to your towns
and cities.

Each day I shine on earth and
warm the air. The warm air rises.
Cooler air pours in and makes the wind.

Swish! Swoosh!
The wind pushes blades
of turbines round and round,
spinning my energy to generators,
which make electricity.

Electricity pours into
copper wires and flows out to
your towns and cities.

Green plants catch my light
and use my energy to help
build leaves and stems.

My energy
builds each bush
and flower, reed and cactus, fruit and tree.
My light fuels all the plants on earth.

Some of the plants are eaten. My energy flows to everything that eats them.

Other plants die and are buried.
Some were buried millions
and millions of years ago
and turned to coal.
Then my energy stayed
deep underground,
locked inside the coal.

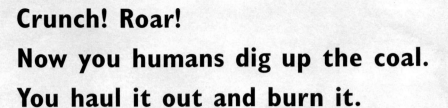

Crunch! Roar!
Now you humans dig up the coal.
You haul it out and burn it.

The fire heats water into steam.
Whoosh!
The steam shoots against
giant turbines, which spin
round and round. They send
my energy to generators,
which make electricity.

From coal-fired power plants,
electricity flows in copper
wires, out to your
towns and cities.

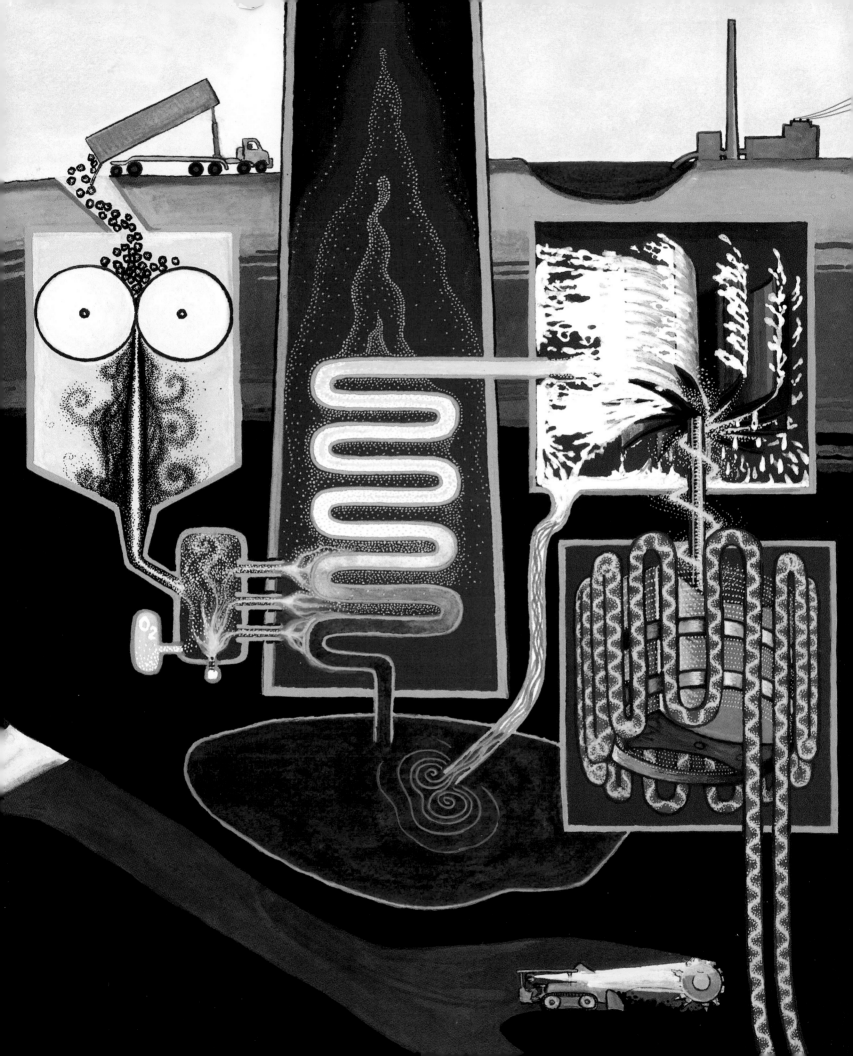

My light falls on solar cells
and charges their electrons.

No turbines, no generators—

electricity streams across the cells,
which pour it into copper wires.

Electricity flows to the building below.

When darkness falls, you turn a switch.

From rushing wind and water,
from burning coal, from silent solar cells,
you let my energy into your room.

Electricity lights the night.

Inside a light bulb,
a wire grows hot.
It glows.

Inside a fluorescent tube,
gas is energized.
It glows.

When you turn on lights at night,
they look like stars have fallen down to earth.

Those lights are energy from me, your golden star,
caught and transformed by your earth,
and by yourselves.

For a moment,
my light illuminates your towns and cities.

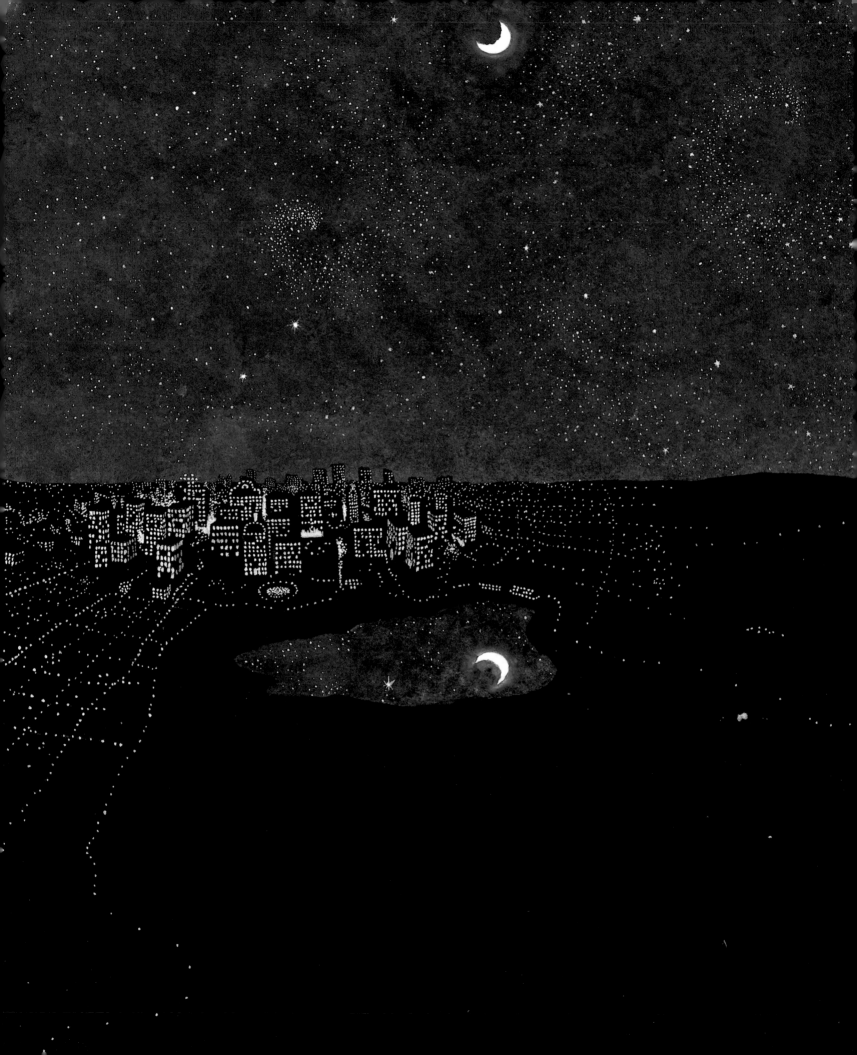

Then, like the starlight from which it came,
it fades back into space.

ABOUT THIS BOOK

For most of my life, I have not been very interested in electricity. I knew it was something that flowed in wires and ran motors and turned on lights, and that was all. I became interested only when I put solar panels on my house, and I wondered how the tiny wires embedded in glass could actually catch sunlight and turn it into energy that powers my stove, water heater, washing machine, computer, TV, and all my lights. This book is part of what I found out.

I guess the main lesson I've learned is that energy constantly changes form, and that humans have learned how to capture these different forms. But we just hold it for a moment. Then the energy passes on.

When I originally wrote the notes for the back of this book, they went on for pages and pages. I felt I had to explain everything I had learned about atoms, dams, coal mining, and everything else in the book. The notes started turning into an encyclopedia, and my editor suggested I cut them _way_ back. Now those notes are on my Web site at www.mollybang.com, and I hope interested readers will do further research on their own.

What follows are a few of the most basic background facts I was thinking about as I made the pictures for <u>My Light</u>.

When we look up at the sky at night, we see stars, the moon, and sometimes a planet or two. But these are only a minute amount of all the matter in the universe. Almost all of the universe seems to be made of what is called "dark matter" and "dark energy," and nobody knows what these are—yet.

But we do know something about the matter that makes up the stars, the moon, and the planets. All this matter is made of tiny particles called <u>atoms</u>. Atoms make up all matter on earth—including ourselves. Atoms have a central nucleus made of protons and neutrons, with electrons spinning around the nucleus.

Hydrogen and helium are two kinds of atoms. As the burning heat of the sun fuses hydrogen atoms together and turns them into helium, they give off energy. This energy travels out into space in all directions as electromagnetic waves—waves of all sizes, from very short to very long. The whole range of these waves is called the <u>electromagnetic spectrum</u>. A tiny portion of these

waves strikes the earth. Light is just the

very small part of the wave spectrum that we can see.

What is electricity? Electricity is a flow of electrons. If only a few electrons flow, we say that is a small electric current. If lots of electrons flow, this is a large current. The larger the current, the bigger the wire needed to carry it.

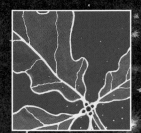

Plants can catch sunlight and use it to break water and carbon dioxide apart and build them into sugar because they contain a chemical in their leaves called <u>chlorophyll</u>. This ability is called <u>photosynthesis</u>—from the Greek for "light putting (things) together." But the plant gives something off when it makes sugar. It gives off oxygen, sending it out into the air, where humans and other animals (and in the darkness, plants) use it to breathe and live.

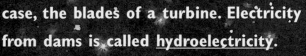

The power from dams comes from the energy released when falling water hits something—in this case, the blades of a turbine. Electricity from dams is called <u>hydroelectricity</u>.

Something was left out of these pictures because they were getting too complicated. I left out the transformers. They should be in between the power lines from the hydroelectric station and the next picture of the wires. Transformers are coils of wires that increase or decrease the voltage or force of electricity:

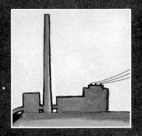

they "transform" the voltage going through wires. Transformers increase the voltage so less is lost when it travels in large wires over long distances. At the other end, transformers decrease the voltage so smaller amounts of electricity can go to each neighborhood in a city.

If much electricity flowed into you, it would badly hurt you or even kill you. The electric wires in your house are insulated. This means they are covered in plastic, which doesn't carry an electric current, so the current can't flow into you.

Lightning is a form of electricity, too. Lightning occurs when the bottoms of clouds become more and more full of negative energy, and the earth's surface becomes more and more positive. Finally, all that negative and positive energy comes together so fast in such a powerful stream, that the air around it explodes. Thunder is the sound of that explosion.

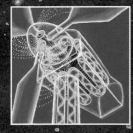

Wind turbines work best where there is a strong, constant wind, such as on tops of low hills or by the sea. The longer the blades and the faster the wind blows, the more electricity they produce. Now "farms" of hundreds of wind turbines have been built and provide enough electricity for whole towns.

Of course trees and bushes are also a fuel that we burn to produce electricity. A few power plants do burn them, but we now use trees mostly for building materials.

Coal is made from ancient plants, so it is called a <u>fossil fuel</u>. The two other fossil fuels are oil and gas. Fossil fuels are made mainly of carbon. They were formed over millions of years, probably by carbon-rich plants and tiny animals getting buried underground and compressed into their new forms.

Solar cells only work when the sun shines, so they are most useful in places where there is lots of sunshine all year long. Also, you need a lot of them to catch enough sunlight to make much power, so they are used on large surfaces, like roofs. Solar cells need batteries to store their energy so we'll still have some when the sun doesn't shine, just as wind turbines need batteries to store their energy for when the wind doesn't blow.

The black boxes in the far left of the picture look like solar cells, but they don't have the grid on them. They are solar water heaters. On their roofs, some people put black

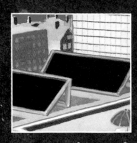

containers full of a liquid antifreeze that heats up in sunlight and is then piped down to a big tank of water. The water gets very hot and is used to wash clothes, dishes, and people, and to heat the house.

Does any of our electricity <u>not</u> come from the sun? Yes. Some of our electricity comes from nuclear energy, which comes from the breakdown of radioactive elements like uranium that are in the ground. Also, geothermal energy is heat from deep in the earth or from underground hot springs. The country of Iceland gets fifteen percent of its electricity from geothermal energy. And a very small amount of energy is made from turbines that are turned by the action of waves and rising and falling tides.

All of these ways we produce electricity have drawbacks. Dams often hold back silt that fertilized downstream land before they were built. Dams also change the downstream ecology, and some prevent fish from swimming back upstream to spawn.

When fossil fuels burn, they give off sulfur, which turns the rain acidic as it falls on lakes, plants, and soil. Water flowing through

old coal mines is highly acidic and kills life downstream. When coal, oil, and gas formed, long before humans existed, there was much more carbon dioxide in the air. As the plants died and became fossil fuels, all the carbon that was in them got buried underground, and the air changed. Now, as we burn fossil fuels,

the carbon floats back into the air and forms carbon dioxide again, which acts like a blanket or a greenhouse, holding more heat than oxygen and warming the air and earth more. It took millions of years to bury the carbon. We are releasing it in only a couple of hundred—very, very, very fast. We do not know what such rapid warming will do. And when fossil fuels burn, they produce tiny particles that get in our lungs and cause us harm.

Wind turbines cause no pollution. They work best in open spaces like low hills or the sea, and these are far from large cities. Much of their electricity is lost as it travels through long power lines to the far-away cities where it is needed. Solar panels don't cause pollution, either. They work best where there is a lot of sun, and they need large flat areas like roofs of low buildings. (The ones in the picture could only make enough electricity for the top floor of the apartment.

They would be better on houses of only one or two stories.) Both wind and solar need storage batteries, so there is still electricity when the wind doesn't blow or the sun doesn't shine. Some states let your extra wind or solar power flow back into the power lines, and they pay you for the power you give back.

As much as we need to discover new and better ways to make electricity, we need to use less of it every day: insulate our houses better, make more energy-efficient appliances and vehicles, turn off lights and other appliances when we aren't using them. Saving electricity and using it wisely are as important as making it.

My Light is based on concepts I learned from Penny Chisholm, a close friend and an ecologist at MIT. It is dedicated to George and Katherine Woodwell and everyone else at the Woods Hole Research Center, for your guidance and persistence and refusal to give up hope. And with many thanks to other heavenly bodies: Jim Green, Phil Sterne, Bonnie Verburg, and Kathy Westray.

THE BLUE SKY PRESS

Library of Congress catalog card number: 2003006960
ISBN 0-439-48961-X
10 9 8 7 6 5 4 3   05 06 07 08
Printed in Singapore   46
First printing, March 2004
Designed by Kathleen Westray